LET ME TALK

THE THOUGHTS OF A BROKEN MAN

JAJUAN MORROW

TABLE OF CONTENTS

DEDICATION

This book is dedicated to my beloved mother, Sharee Brown. Our relationship is one I deeply cherish. From our long phone calls to the memories we've created, I am so thankful for this newfound bond we share. We laugh, we joke, and we continue to grow closer—thank you for being such an important part of my life.

To my angel, my brother, Michael Sample: I am my brother's keeper. Though I'm learning to live this life without you physically here, I carry you with me every day. Keep watching over us because I still need you.

To my baby sister, Myesha Sample: My My, you will always be my baby sister, and I will always have your back no matter what life throws at us. It's us against the world.

To my sons, Mik'heal and Jajuan Morrow jr: I love you more than words can express. I am pushing through this darkness to make you proud. Always remember—Dada loves you. You are my reason for never giving up!

I wish we had forever, but since we didn't, I'd like to take this moment to dedicate this book to you as well, my father, Christopher Morrow Sr. God called you home before we could mend what was broken, but I want to say it now: I forgive you. I am becoming a better man each and every day, and I carry that growth with me in your memory.

INTRODUCTION

They say men aren't supposed to cry. We're told to keep our pain buried, to never show vulnerability because the world might see it as weakness. From an early age, I learned to silence my emotions, to wear a mask of strength while the weight of my pain crushed me from the inside.

Before a woman ever hurt me, I was broken by my *FATHER*—the man who was supposed to protect me. As a child, I endured the sting of my father's beatings, each strike leaving more than just physical bruises. They left wounds on my soul, shaping a boy who would grow into a man with so much to say but no one willing to listen.

Love and hurt have walked hand in hand in my life, inseparable companions that have shaped my journey. I've loved deeply, been hurt profoundly, and carried the scars of those experiences in silence. At my lowest, I even contemplated ending it all, believing there was no escape from the darkness that consumed me.

But this book is my escape. Let Me Talk is my chance to say the words I've carried in my heart for years—the words my mouth was never allowed to speak. It's for every man who has ever felt unheard, unseen, or told that his pain isn't valid.

To my fellow men, know this: we can cry. We can hurt. We can be vulnerable without it diminishing our strength or our worth. This is not a sign of weakness—it's a sign of being human.

So, dive deep into my story. These pages hold the raw truth of my life—the pain, the love, the anger, the healing. This is not just my story; it's the story of countless men who've been told to suffer in silence.

This time, I'm speaking. And I hope you'll listen.

Broken Memories

Broken Memories

It's 5:15 AM, and I've been awoken by another dream. My dreams are starting to come more often than before. I don't know if it's because this time last year I was a wreck, or if it's intuition. I've had these same dreams before; it's like I can see things in my dreams that I can't see in reality, or is it my brother warning me of upcoming battles, trying to prepare me for the unthinkable? Only God knows. I don't trust anything that breathes air. I stopped believing in people because everyone has a hidden agenda. What a life to live, not knowing who to trust or who really loves you, and who just wants you around because of your passion for helping others. They say what you go through only makes you stronger, but that's not always true because some things you go through damage you from the inside out, leaving you broken with a smile, or leaving you with haunting images or thoughts in your head that keep coming back. No matter what, they stay. I hate going through certain things in life because it makes it hard for me to move on. Throughout my life, I've given my love and trust to all the wrong people.

It all started with my dad. All my life, I wanted this man to be there. I loved him with all of me, even though I didn't know him. I remember when he first came back into my life; I was at Heart Grove Mental Hospital, placed there by my mother after I tried to set the house on fire with me in it. That night, I lit the stove, put a half-empty pot on the eye, and laid on the couch to sleep, not wanting to feel anything. I had made up my mind that life would be better without me. I remember being awoken by the screams and hollers of my mother as she walked into a home full of smoke. She was fussing and screaming, snatching me off the couch, asking, "What are you doing? Are you trying to set the building on fire?" I had no answers, so I just stared at her as she went on about how I needed help, and she was getting me some.

I remember hearing the ambulance approaching, and when they arrived, my mother explained to them that she thought I had tried to commit suicide and wanted to seek immediate help. They loaded me into the back of the ambulance, and the next thing I knew, I was at Heart Grove Mental Institute, locked in a room once again, alone. As the days went by— meeting after meeting, group after group—I became worse, not because I was crazy, but because, like I had always felt, I felt abandoned and alone. I tried crying; that didn't work. I even tried fighting to relieve some of my pain, but that only got me a needle in the butt and abuse from the hospital nurses. I never told anyone, but mental hospitals are not for kids. They say they're restraining you, but what restraint comes with punches? I never heard of restraint that came with choking or a knee to the ribs, but in everyone's eyes, this was what I needed.

I remember calling home one day, and my mother said to me, "Your dad is here and wants you to come live with him." Oh man, I was so excited! In my head, I thought I had finally been rescued. My dad had finally come to get me; I thought my life was about to change. Little did I know, it was— but for the worse. I remember the day my dad and mom came to visit. When I saw him, my world lit up. Finally, I was going with my dad; I would finally have the fatherly love that I saw my siblings receive daily. I remember the conversation we had—he asked how I was, why I was acting out, and why I would do what I had done. I didn't give him a real answer; I was just ready to escape this one-sided home I was living in.

So, after a few days, I was released. I remember him coming to my mom's house to get me. He was full of joy, and seeing this made me feel as if life had just taken a turn for the better. All my lonely days had finally come to an end. I wouldn't have to fight for attention because this was my dad, and I was his son. I had seen how my siblings' father was in their lives, so I figured it was my turn to receive that same love from mine. I remember going to my aunt's house on the South Side of Chicago with him, where we stayed for a couple of days. It felt so good. Everywhere we went, people would tell my dad how much I looked like him and how we were a spitting image of each other. That felt good; I finally felt like I belonged.

I remember getting on the bus headed to his home, which was located in Detroit. He told me all the plans he had for us and how I had siblings who couldn't wait to meet me. My dad was married, had two new children and a stepdaughter, a wife, a home, and a business. Upon arriving in his city, we were greeted by his wife and the kids. She welcomed me with open arms; she was so nice and told me all the things I could do while there. She explained how there were a lot of children my age around their home. After a few minutes, we arrived at my new home. As I exited the car, I looked on in amazement. My dad explained how I had my own room and how he would take me shopping for new clothes. He told me all the things a kid would want to hear. I just wish he would have told me the price it would cost to have all these things.

For the next couple of days, we became close. We went to the mall; he bought me clothes and shoes, even brought home a dog. But I noticed that something wasn't right with him. During the days I had been there, I noticed that he had a quick temper and that he and my stepmother were not on the best of terms. I noticed the drinking, and how when he was mad, he was furious. If you got in his way, he'd run you over. He had a decent hand game and could fight.

I remember the first day I saw his inner rage. I was sitting in the front room when he and my stepmother began arguing. I heard the slap across her face, which caused me to turn and look. They were fighting over drinking and something her brother had said. I remember watching him beat her to the point where she couldn't go outside because of the swelling in her face. I sat and watched as her brother appeared, and my dad stepped on the porch to remind him of how badly he would beat him. They argued for what felt like hours—there was nonstop bumping, nonstop hollering—and then it just went silent. My dad came back down from his room, sweating and out of breath. He looked at me, and I remember looking into his eyes; you could see the rage, and you could also smell the liquor. It was clear he was not in his right state of mind.

He left that night and told me he would be back. I fell asleep waiting for him, but little did I know I would soon see that same rage coming toward me. I remember waking up the next day to the sounds of The Isley Brothers' "Voyage to Atlantis" blaring from the stereo. My dad was up moving around as usual. When I came down the stairs, I saw him sitting on the couch holding my little sister. He looked up at me, and I could tell something was wrong. Instead of bothering him, I went to the kitchen, grabbed food, and went out to sit on the porch.

While sitting on the porch, enjoying my donut and cereal, I saw two kids playing in the lot next to our home. They saw me and began to approach. I don't remember their names, but I do remember that it was a girl and a boy. They approached and asked if I would like to join them in a game of hide and seek. I agreed to play and asked my stepmother if I could join them in the lot. She said yes and told me to be careful.

After playing for a while, I learned that they lived behind my father's house and had seen me there before with him but hadn't had the chance to meet me. As we talked, we grew closer. They would come over every day to get me, and we would run up and down the street all day. When night fell, we'd sit on my back porch until their grandmother called for them to come in for dinner. One day, while playing, they asked if I had tried a cigarette. I said no. They then asked if my dad smoked. I said yes, and then they asked if I could get one of his cigarettes so we could try it. I agreed; I just wish I had known that that one cigarette would open a door that would change my life forever.

As I approached the front door once again, I could hear my dad's music. When I opened the door to the house, my dad was once again sitting in the front room, music blaring, and it was dark. The only reason I could see him was because of a small opening in the curtains that allowed a tiny glimmer of sunlight in. When I closed the door behind me, he looked up and said, "Come here, son." I sat by him, and he explained how much he loved me and cared for me. He told me that real men provide for and protect their family at all costs. We began to play wrestle, and then he started to teach me boxing techniques and how to defend myself. I was having so much fun that I forgot about the mission at hand: getting a cigarette.

After a while of sparring with my dad, my stepmom called him upstairs. I thought, "What a better time to steal one," so I went into his box and took a Newport. After getting the cigarette, I went to the beginning of the stairs. I could hear them still arguing, so I decided I would just holler up to let them know I was leaving to join my friends.

As I began toward the front door, I could hear the furniture moving in their room, followed by screams, and arguing. I was a child, so I paid no attention and headed out the door. I caught up with my friends and felt like I had just accomplished something by getting the cigarette, so I was in a rush to show them. We found a little hiding spot; I lit the cigarette with a lighter I had stolen from my dad and took a puff. I immediately began to cough, so I passed it to my friends. They each took a puff, and like me, they began to cough from the strength of the tobacco. I remember my dad coming to the back porch, calling my name. I ran to the house so fast because you could tell by the way he was calling me that something was wrong. I was so nervous when I approached him; I just knew I had been caught. But he smiled when he saw me and said I had to come in. I said okay and opened the gate to enter our yard.

I remember walking into the house; my dad was standing by the stairs. He said to me, "Come here." As I walked toward him, something didn't feel right. For some reason, I felt a bad vibe coming from him. His eyes were so red, and you could tell he was still angry. The veins in his head bulged, and the way his jaw muscles tightened—it's like the closer I got to him, the more fear came over me.

When I finally stood in front of him, he asked, "Did you steal a cigarette out of my box?" Like any kid, I replied, "No." A smirk came over his face—one that I had seen before. It wasn't a happy smirk; every time I saw this expression on his face, he was angry, so I knew this wasn't going to end well. He began to ask me if I thought I was a man. I replied, "No." He then asked if I thought he was my mother. I said, "No." At that point, he swung. I had never been hit like that. The pressure in that punch buckled my knees. I fell to the ground, but he instantly stood me back up and repeated his question: "Do you think you're a man?" I responded "No" again. That "no" was followed by numerous punches and slaps from my father. While enduring that pain, I couldn't help but think, "All this for a cigarette?"

After what seemed like forever, he instructed me to go clean myself up; he had busted my lip and made the mistake of hitting me in the eye, which caused it to swell. As I sat in the bathroom, wiping the blood away, I cried. I couldn't understand why he would beat me so badly for something so small. My dad came to the washroom and began to tell me how sorry he was, that he was just trying to raise me to be a man, and that he noticed when I left to go play, his cigarettes had been turned a different way than he had left them. I apologized and continued to clean myself. He told me he loved me and, when I was done, to go to bed—and that's just what I did.

The next morning, I awoke with a swollen face and a black eye. I went to my stepmother and told her I wanted to call my mom. She suggested that wouldn't be a good idea and told me not to let my father hear me say that. I begged and told her to look at my face. She told me to remain quiet so my father wouldn't hear me. Little did I know, it was too late. My dad had overheard our conversation and was already planning his next attack. I'll never forget how I felt that day when I heard him call out to me to come downstairs. I was so scared because, for some reason, I knew this was not a good call.

As I approached the last step, my father approached and said to me, "You can call your mother all you want. She can't save you. I'm your father, and you live with me now." He instructed me to go get everything he had bought me—shoes, clothes, etc. I immediately went to my room to gather the belongings he had purchased. When I returned to the stairs leading down to the front room, I could see him pacing across the floor, mad with rage. I began to walk down toward him slowly. He looked up, and as I approached the last step, he asked, "You think you're a man?"

I replied, "No." He then asked, "Do you think your mom can protect you?" I didn't reply; I just stared. I was so scared; my heart was beating so fast because I knew this wasn't going to end well. When he began to approach me, I started looking for ways out. I noticed he had the backdoor open, and my mind began to race. All I could think was, "I need to call my mother." So I dashed toward the door. He chased me, but I made it out. I ran down the alley so fast. I remembered a payphone he had once used that wasn't too far from his house. I ran straight there.

When I finally got to the phone, I tried calling my mother, but there was no answer. I called back; still no answer. Now I was panicking because I knew my dad was not far behind me. I called my grandmother, and on the second ring, she answered. I began telling her what my dad had done, how he had beaten me and was about to do it again, so I ran away to a payphone to call her. My grandmother had a fit; she told me to hold on while she contacted my mother. But while waiting for her to click back over, I could hear a dog chain hitting the concrete. I looked back, and there was my dad coming toward me once again—eyes red, jaw tight, and a chain wrapped in his fist. I screamed as loud as I could into the phone, hoping my grandmother would click in before he reached me.

As soon as she did, I could hear my mom say, "What's going on, son?" and then the phone went dead. My father had hung up on them. In such a panic, I hadn't paid attention to how close he really was. He struck me with a blow to the face. I fell. He picked me up and began carrying me back home. I kicked and screamed for help, but no one tried to rescue me. I pleaded with my father, but even he had become deaf to my pleas.

As we approached the home, I remember him saying to me, "I'm going to kill your little ass. You think it's a game?" Truth be told, I thought he was going to do just that. When we finally got to the house and entered through the back door, he slammed me on the floor and began punching and kicking me. I could hear his wife screaming, asking him to stop, but the beating continued. After about 10 minutes of kicks and punches, he grabbed me and dragged me to the front room and told me to sit on the couch and not say a thing—and that's what I did.

As the day went on, I sat there without saying a word. I remember thinking to myself that I'd never let someone hurt me like this again. I'd never let anyone get close enough to bring bodily harm; most of all, I'd never trust again. As I sat there deep in thought, I heard someone beating on the door.

I peeked out the window and saw my mom. My dad asked, "Who is it?" and opened the door. My mom entered and walked right past me. Due to the swelling, she couldn't tell it was me; she just walked past. I called out to her, and when she turned around, it broke her heart. There I was, sitting with a swollen face, black eyes, and blood on my shirt. She ran to me and grabbed me, saying, "I got you, and I'm so sorry"—and we exited my dad's house. As we got in the car, he stood on the porch going back and forth with my mom. Who would have known that would be the last time I saw him alive?

Since that day, I've never really trusted people. I became very distant. I didn't allow anyone to get close to me. Love was just a four-letter word with no meaning.

DROWNING IN MY OWN TEARS

Aug 19 – DROWNING IN MY OWN TEARS

Why is it that when men speak, our words fall upon deaf ears? Why are our sentences silenced? Why are our hurts never acknowledged, and our pains never healed? Why do we suffer from being children of absent fathers? Why are our mental emotions so much weaker than our physical strengths? As a boy, I never paid attention to the cries of a man, but now that I am a man, I cry the same tears that I have seen on so many men's faces. Not the physical tears, but the hidden tears—the over-drinking, the over-abuse of substances, the days and nights of no sleep, the feeling of being in a room full of people yet still feeling alone, the thoughts of giving up but not being able to because you have to be strong for your family, the not knowing where you fit in.

I have seen these tears so many times on men's faces in my life, and I never knew what they were going through. A battle with life is what some might call it, but in reality, it's really a battle with death. So many men walk around daily living in the flesh but dying mentally and emotionally on the inside, and it's sad because most men keep fighting. Not because they are scared of the thought of death, but because, even though life is miserable and very exhausting, they continue to think of the ones whose their absence would hurt. So they dwell in this agony of pain and hurt just to not hurt the ones they love. They continue to endure the pain, still not being noticed or heard.

So, is this the role of a man? To protect and not be protected? To listen and not be heard? Or is it to love and never receive love in return? Or better yet, is it to sacrifice everything they have, even their lives, as long as they provide happiness for those they love? Deep, right? But ask yourself this: How deep does it have to go before there's no return?

Imagine drowning at the beach, and the same people you once helped pull out of the water stand on shore with ropes in hand and watch you drown. Now that's a deep hurt! The crazy part about this is that the whole time, you knew how to swim but forgot due to the hurt that overtook you from watching the ones you love watch you drown!

So, in reality, it wasn't the waves from the strong current that overtook you; it was hurt that actually drowned you—drowning in your own tears.
Why Not?

Nobody understands you when your feelings are hurting. They don't even accept that they play a major part in your ongoing pain. To lose it all is one of the hardest things I've faced. I've lost my freedom, my home, my family, and all the while going through this devastating part of life, I still manage to smile and show love to everyone around me. I still manage to put on a smile.

February 14, 2024, my world turned upside down. My emotions took over me; I became so full of hurt that I made a drastic decision, and it cost me everything: my job, my trucking school, my freedom, my family, my sanity, and my mind. It cost me everything but my life, and I don't even want that. How do you fight for something you don't want? I pray for death, and my prayers are never answered. They say God hears you when you pray, but why not grant me my wishes? Why let me dwell in the hurt as if I have no one—not even my kids?

Why continue to let me suffer in this life? I no longer want a life; I no longer want to live. Why not give me the peace I ask for? Why not end my suffering and pain? Why continue to watch me battle daily, hurting daily, creating daily, longing for the one thing He will not grant me? I miss my brother. I miss my granny. They used to know what to say on days I felt down, the days I felt like giving up. My granny used to say, "Not so! Keep fighting." My brother used to say, "Make better decisions, big bro!"

I feel as though I'm being punished for my past life or that I'm being shown what I made so many others feel. I'm homeless. I'm lonely. I'm defeated, with no way out. I can honestly say I know what the bottom feels like. It's dark. It's draining. It's hurtful. It snatches life out of you and makes life feel like death in reverse. But what does death feel like?

HOOD NIGGA

HOOD NIGGA

For years, I've always put myself last and never first. I've always wanted more for those around me, never pushing myself to be great. I've been stabbed in the back; I've even had my joy stripped away, and I still never turned my back on people. I always kept it, as they say, "100". I may have dipped and dabbled a lot in my life, but not once did I break or run from anyone I truly loved.

Being a misunderstood person is hard because no one really takes the time to truly understand you. Most will use you; some will love you only from a distance, and some will just degrade and judge you—not based on who you are as a person, but based on what you can provide for them.

For example, I'm a street-raised guy, and every woman wants a guy like me who has that "hood" in him, but most women don't even know how to love that type of man. Believe it or not, men are battered too; we have endured pain, been taken for granted, and used. We have loved the wrong person before; our hearts do break, our thoughts can overwhelm us, and they get the best of our minds. We are broken individuals with a survival mindset and a "trust no one" mentality.

Most men that you see in the streets are not there because it was their first choice in life; most are there because there's a void in their hearts they're trying to fill. This void leads them to the streets or to the arms of your neighborhood gang or drug dealer. It's love; every man, just like every woman, wants to be loved. He wants a family; he wants a wife; he wants kids; he wants everything he never had at home.

Now, when dealing with this man, you're going to have to be a strong and careful woman because, although he may want everything I mentioned, he is still going to be very unaccepting of your love and truths. Even though this is what he longs for, he doesn't know how to accept it or allow himself to embrace it. The streets have taught him a different way of love and how it's expressed. His trust will be hard to gain due to numerous disappointments. He's going to put you through every test; he might even hurt you with violent outbursts or hurtful words that cut to your core, but this is what he knows.

A fact about a hood guy is that we tend to have more love for our homies than for our women. I know you're thinking, "What? I'm his woman; he lays with me every night, we have kids together." The truth is none of this really matters. Let me explain.

When most guys decide to go to the streets, it's either because money is needed for their family, and they feel they have to do this in order to provide, or because they were hard-headed growing up and no one in their family really cared for them. So, they go and create a family, and most of the time, that family consists of local drug dealers or gangs.

Now, we both know there isn't really any love in the streets; there's disloyalty, hate, and constant physical and mental abuse. So, we hold on tightly to those closest to us, which are our homies and family. When it comes to relationships, most hood dudes don't take them seriously at first because most females that want a hood dude only want his money, protection, or the security of being with someone everyone respects due to his street credibility.

While growing up in the streets, men run through girlfriends like clothing. Most girls don't know what they want while growing up, but when you take a man who doesn't know love and show him a false presentation of what love is, it not only damages him but also pushes his belief in the word "love" farther and farther away. So, he goes right back to those who he knows really love him: his hood family, his homies.

So, while a woman may say, "I love a hood nigga," the question is: can you still love that hood nigga when the hood comes out of him toward you? Can you love this damaged man? Can you continue to guide him toward better when he's drifting toward worse? And the biggest question of all is: if he gave you his heart, could you carry it and show him that there is such a thing as love without becoming a recurring disappointment? Before you get to that man's heart, he's going to put you through hell.

Ask yourself, can I understand the pain he's going to put me through or why he's going to put me through it? It's a battle that most aren't ready for.

SILENT TEARS

SILENT TEARS

These silent tears I cry are the hardest ever. Although tears may swell up in my eyes, they are forced not to shed, and the words that explain are left unsaid due to a lack of communication and prejudged blame. As I sit, my heart burns with intense fire, and my mind begins to wander. Soon, I become engulfed in thoughts that make the pain even worse. My breathing becomes heavy due to a rising outcry, but I choose to muffle it with either liquor or weed, hoping that what usually makes me happy can tend to this brokenness that I have been forced to put off once again.

Can I be heard? They say a closed mouth doesn't get fed, but what about a mouth that opens and has no voice? What am I to do when all I'm asking for is an ear and a little understanding of my feelings and outlooks on situations that affect me? I've learned that communication is crucial in a relationship, as is listening and understanding; these three things I've found to be an issue. But am I allowed to say this? Am I allowed to speak my mind without offense being taken or attitudes changing? Can I voice what hurts me?

I feel as though no matter what I do or say, I'm forever going to be the bad guy, even when my intentions are good and I'm truly coming to the conversation with an open mind, willing to understand. No man wants to feel like he doesn't belong, or that if he voices his opinion, he will lose his family or revisit a part of past experiences.

What a life to live—a life where you have to stay quiet due to the fear of losing someone. What a life to live, going day to day unheard! What a life to live, knowing that everyone hates you and is firm in their verdict about you. What a life to live when you're living in paradise and feeling like it's a rainy day. What a life to live not knowing if you're good enough or if someone really loves you. What a life to live, changing everything about yourself on every level just to feel it's not appreciated.

I know that life throws curveballs, and in relationships and marriages, those balls never stop coming. But I'm also learning that it's not the ball that's thrown; it's the batter's judgment on which one he should swing at. Only the batter knows which ball is thrown right. He makes the decision on when to swing and when not to swing. Life is like a baseball game; you have all these fans—some on your side, some not—and they're waiting to see if you strike out or hit a home run.

In relationships, we tend to forget about our team and focus on pleasing the fans. But without the team, how do you win the game? You don't; you continue to lose. There will be no playoffs, and there will be no World Series. Why? Because you chose to play for the onlookers instead of playing for the ones who really want you to win—and that's your team. There should be no reason for silent cries in relationships because I have cried my last.

WHO AM I?

WHO AM I?

I am Jajuan Lamont Morrow, son of Sharee Brown and Christopher Darnell Morrow. I am a child of pain, both physical and mental. I am broken by so many years of hurt, carrying around a heavy burden of built-up pain. I am misunderstood; to know what I feel is to walk in my shoes, but to truly understand me, you would have to listen. I am held back by my own fears, my disbeliefs, and my lack of trust in people. I am stuck in an ongoing battle within my mind, which sometimes gets the best of me.

I am a man who doesn't know where he stands in life. I am a man with good intentions and ideals but with a lack of self-motivation. I am a man whose mind never stops; I am a think tank. I am a man who is just trying to figure out life— a man with dreams and many things I want to accomplish, yet I am held back by my own insecurities. I am a man who is haunted by his past and afraid of his future.

WHY AM I WHERE I AM TODAY, THIS MINUTE?

Why Am I Where I Am Today, This Minute?

I am where I am today because the life I chose to live, and my younger choices laid out in some way how my future would be.

How Do I Feel About My Identity?

I feel like I'm a good person. I feel like I'm a pawn to people. I feel like I wouldn't matter if I weren't beneficial to others.

What Have I Quit Hoping For?

I have quit hoping for peace and happiness. I've tried in so many ways to achieve these two goals, and I've failed each time. Each attempt has only hurt me with false hope, or I might feel like I've found it only for it to be destroyed, leaving me to rebuild myself alone and in pain. I'm tired of hurting myself with false hope. I'm tired of forcing myself to be happy while feeling down or wondering when I'll feel my next pain, my next hurt. So, I decided too just live.

Have You Ever Felt Unappreciated or Overlooked? Even by the ones you love?

All the time, I feel as if no one appreciates me and all that I try to do. I feel like no one sees all that I sacrifice or the sacrifices I've made. I feel like no one truly accepts me for who I am. I feel as if everybody around me has an agenda, and I say this because no one ever talks about what I've done to change; they only dwell on my past and how I was. No one speaks about the moves I've made to become a better son, a better husband, a better father, a better listener, or a calm head. No one ever acknowledges how

I've changed or how happy they are with me or for me. I've just come to realize that no matter how hard you try, people are never going to see you for who you're becoming; they only see what you were or find ways to use your past against you.

What Pressures Are Tearing at Your Heart and Life Right Now?
Am I a good father? Am I doing right by my kids?
Am I a good husband? Is my wife truly happy with me?
Will I succeed in my business ventures?
Can I let my guard down? Can I open my heart and give my all, including trust?

What Are You Like When Depressed or Discouraged?
I'm quiet for the most part, off to myself in thought. I'm angered and very moody; my temper is sometimes more than I can bear. I can be disrespectful and very violent. I'm basically in a state of giving up or have a "don't care" attitude.

Who Are You in the Dark?
I feel evil and very aggressive. My body grows hot inside like a volcano ready to erupt. My thoughts become those of a madman with a thirst to hurt. I become more impatient, and my tolerance for anything is beyond low. My mind wanders, and I begin to think of all my hurts and pains: the backstabs, the disloyalty, the false hope. I become full of rage, fighting to hold in what's threatening to come out, with a mind racing with painful thoughts and a heart that's literally shattered. I become a human bomb.

How Do You Handle Pressure and Loss?

This depends on the situation and the pressure being applied. Everyday life can be hard to deal with. I'm a father and husband who has to provide for my family, but it can be overwhelming. To not have a father and then have to be a father is a task of its own; you're learning patience as well as control. Loss has always been a problem for me.

My Strengths and Liabilities

Strengths:
- Willpower
- Protective
- Helper
- Ability to create
- Dedication
- Love
- Kind heart
- Thinking

Liabilities:
- Temper
- Thoughts
- Rage
- Not speaking my mind
- Faith
- Trust

- Believing in people

- Not believing in myself

- Letting go and not holding on

- Fitting in with the crowd

Who Will I Be If I Fail?

A man without direction, a man with no true meaning in life. Uneducated, with no hope and a background filled with past mistakes. A man searching for who he wants to be, with no idea of who he should be. A father who can't raise men because he himself feels less than what he's trying to teach them to be. A lost cause with no hope for the future. I'd be just a man, a human. I'd just be living with no purpose—just a body with no heart and mind.

LET ME TALK!

LET ME TALK!

Women and men, stop saying, "I've changed for her" or "I've changed for him." Stop forcing yourself to become someone else's idea of who you should be. Stop belittling yourself because your partner might have an opinion on who or what you should be. I say this because most of the time, you are pushing yourself to be this perfect individual, trying to become exactly what your partner has requested. However, your partner wasn't even prepared to accept all the changes you presented simply because they asked for something they couldn't handle. The reason they can't handle you is that they never changed anything about themselves to complement the new you.

Ask yourself this: How many people go to a car lot, pick the best car, knowing they can't afford it? Or how many people do you know who pray for the perfect job, obtain it, and then quit? This happens because most of the time, they asked for more than they are prepared to take care of, and they are not prepared because they never took a step toward changing themselves.

So, change for you. Change because you want better. Change because you think your life will flourish. Change because you want it. When you do it for yourself, it lasts a lifetime.

Thinking:

While sitting and thinking, a certain subject came to mind: Why is it that a person could choose not to deal with you but not allow you to be with what builds you up? Would they rather see you struggling than getting by? Why does it hurt them to see you happy? Is that love?

HELLO, SYCO

Sometimes you have to return to who you were in order to become who you are trying to be. I guess it's time to let him back out.

Hello, Syco

I'm going to let you out for just a small amount of time. I'm sorry I had to put you away; I was trying to be someone different. I was trying to become normal and live a peaceful life, but I see they don't want peace. Everyone has a role in this world, and you, my friend, have always been there on those nights when I had no one. On those nights when I was alone, you gave me the strength to get through. I always knew I wouldn't fit into this perfect life.

As soon as you start to show weakness, the enemy attacks and beats you, and I'm tired of getting beaten. I'm tired of being soft. I'm tired of being nice—fuck that. I've learned that being emotional only gets you hurt. Do you remember when we first met? I was lying on the floor, beaten. I had no strength; I couldn't see. I was scared and didn't know a way out. That day, you came and comforted me. You taught me to be aware, you taught me to absorb pain, and most of all, you taught me how not to feel. I became the predator; I was no longer prey.

And here I am again, feeling like prey because I've allowed myself to love. Yeah, I fell in love. It was nice at first; she was the coolest person in the world, my ride or die. Yeah, I remember (don't trust anyone), but it felt so real. I did what you said: I put her through tests and waited a long time before I gave her my heart. I didn't trust her at first, but I gave in. Ten years together, and I figured this was it for me. But once again, my weakness has gotten the best of me. I turned my back on you. I moved to different states. I no longer allowed you to show yourself, but you are free today, my friend, and I'll never put you away again for anybody. Promise!!

BOTH WAYS

Hurt
Goes
Both Ways

BOTH WAYS

I'm sitting here; it's 3:15 AM, and I can't sleep. Life just feels so odd to me. I've been trying to watch TV, but my mind won't let me. My head feels heavy due to all the random thoughts racing through my mind.

Have you ever wanted to be in love but your scared to let your guard down to allow the love to be received and your heart to be given? Or have you ever sat up while your partner slept, watching them, and thinking to yourself, "Damn, I love you and hate you at the same time?" What about those days when they might say something or move a certain way that sets off unwanted memories?

I've got one better: have you ever sat back in your feelings, looked at your partner, and said to yourself, "Damn, this is what it feels like?" Or have you ever asked yourself, "Am I man or woman enough to deal with this like he or she did?" And if not, why do I feel so connected to this person? Why do I feel so connected on certain days and distant on others? Is it because of the fear of misguided love? Or is it because you're afraid of feeling that pain again? That pain that broke you, that made you feel like life didn't even matter? That pain that not only broke your heart but your mind as well? That pain that keeps you up at night while everyone sleeps, that "let me get a fifth of Remy and two packs of Backwoods for the half you just bought" pain?

The crazy part about all the pain you're feeling—the hurt you're carrying, the trust issues, the feelings of betrayal, etc.—is that you once caused these same feelings in someone's life before. If not with the man or woman you're with now, they have felt these same feelings from you.

(Food for Thought)

Hurt goes both ways.

DEEP THOUGHTS

DEEP THOUGHTS

Where am I heading in life? I'm sitting here thinking, "Damn, I'm 36 with five kids, two grandkids, and a wife. I'm living in a beautiful city; money is cool, and life's great." So why do I feel empty? I'm so confused about what direction I'm going in and how I'm going to start down the path. All I know is that I want to be successful and achieve all my goals. I want to be the best father, the best husband, and the best version of myself. I love who I'm becoming—my level head, the way I respond to unwanted situations. I feel like I can finally be me. I feel like I'm free; I can finally enjoy life and all it has to offer.

Losing my brother was a hard hit for me, but it was also an eye-opener. Losing someone so lovable, someone who wouldn't hurt a fly, made me realize how truly blessed I was. I had to make a change. Then, on top of that, my granny had just passed. Pulling up to her house and seeing them bringing her out broke my heart. But to get into that van and see the man pull the sheet back for me to see her lying there, no longer with us, tore my heart out. Hearing my mother's loud cries screaming, "No, Lord, not my momma," broke me. This pain, while everybody else was able to release, I held in. I cried silently; I held in the screams, I held back the tears. I became unstable, full of so much hurt, so much pain. I became distant; I became enraged.

I started smoking lots of weed, trying to bandage a broken heart and slow down a racing mind. But no matter what I did, I couldn't bear the pain. Then came the disruption in my home life. I had never felt so abandoned. To see my family ride past me, not knowing that at that moment that would be my last time seeing them for a while, shattered me. I felt like my world had just ended; I felt like I was losing everyone I truly loved with all my heart. I didn't know if my wife was coming back or who she was with. I grabbed my car keys and left, going to the liquor store to buy a pint of Hennessy. I began to drink, crying, mad, confused. I knew that I wasn't myself, but I didn't know it was this bad; I thought I had it all under control. But in reality, I didn't.

As I drove up and down the highway at dangerous speeds, I began to think, "Why? Why would she leave me? What had I done?" She had left me for someone else, and as I thought about it, I became enraged with hurt and pain, feeling betrayed. Everyone was calling my phone, except for the one person I wanted to hear from. After driving around for a while, and finally done with the liquor I had purchased, I returned home. I remember sitting on the couch looking at our wedding photo, crying. I began to walk through the house, ranting and raging, because now my mind had won—and the liquor was making my blood boil. All I could think was, "Is she with that guy?" I remember throwing an ashtray out the front window due to being drunk and angry, and I kicked my TV. After that, I had a total blackout.

I remember my aunt waking me up, telling me, "Son, come on, it's time to go." When I opened my eyes, all I could see were the damages I had done, and I thought to myself, "Damn, I fucked up." I remember talking to my wife that day, and she asked me why I would tear the house apart like that. I couldn't give her an answer.

I began to plead with her, asking where she was or who she was with. I was so scared, given our current situation, that she had left me for another guy.

I couldn't focus. Nightmares came every night; everything reminded me of her. I felt like I had lost half of myself, if not most of me. Then my wife called one day and said she was in another state. Now I was really tweaking. She began to explain how we needed this time apart and that I should get help and work on myself, and she would do the same. At the time, I didn't trust a word she was saying. I felt like she just wanted freedom to do her own thing, but I agreed with doubt.

At first, it was hard not talking to the person I was so in love with, but I began to think: What pushed her away? Was it my bad temper? Was it the fighting? Was this payback for all the things I had done? I began to look at myself—my own faults and actions. I wasn't the perfect man either; I had hurt this woman so many times with lies, getting caught up, and on top of that, the physical altercations. I began to think back to all the times I had hurt her, all the times she cried, all the times she begged and pleaded.

What was the difference between what I had done and what she had done? There was none. I realized at that point that hurt goes both ways. I had finally felt what she had been feeling for years. I finally felt the abandonment; I felt what it was like not to know my place. I had a chance to experience what it felt like to catch someone up that I was in love with. Yes, I finally felt how it was to have my heart broken—not just broken, but shattered.

It made me realize how much pain my wife had endured due to my actions. Could I blame her for wanting to get away? No. I told myself I was going to get my act together and read self-help books. I began rebuilding myself. We as men rarely look at our faults; instead, we cover them up with excuses and lies of deceit. We feel, as long as it's a secret, it's okay. But is it okay if she does it? After being separated for six months, my wife and I decided it was time to return to being a couple. She felt I had grown, as well as she had, so we decided it was time to reconnect.

I was excited and scared at the same time. I didn't know what to expect because at this point, I was still in love with her but doubted her intentions. I had so many people telling me that she'd moved on and was comfortable without me—that she'd gotten what she needed and now wanted me back. I would be lying if I said they didn't get into my head. My wife and I had discussed this move on plenty of occasions, but the closer it got, the more I feared going to her. The thoughts of her being with someone else bothered me. I started thinking irrational thoughts—like what if she was "doing her own thing"? How would I know? What if she had slept with someone down there? Is this real? Are we really going to make this work?

During our separation, we had discussed going to an island with some of her friends, where we would sit down and clear the air. Afterward, we would leave all the hurts and pains there. I agreed to the trip, thinking it would help our marriage by giving us some time alone to really talk.

I flew to the new city where we would be staying, and upon arrival, she met me at the airport. To be honest, I didn't know what to expect. I didn't truly trust her. When I got to the car, she jumped out, gave me a kiss, and said, "I missed you." The joy that ran through me was electric, but I still didn't know what she had been up to. So I proceeded with caution. She had booked a nice hotel with a kitchen and an amazing view. We, along with our kids, enjoyed ourselves. We went to the pools, and my wife and I stepped out to hit the local malls. The makeup sex was great, but why was I still feeling like I didn't know where my place was?

The next day, we began to pack, preparing for our flight later that day. She took the kids to her parents, and we headed for the airport. As all men do, I noticed a change in her—the way she dressed, how she smoked weed, how comfortable she had become living in this new state. Some things I liked about the change, like how she kept herself up, how she was more girly, more feminine. I also noticed how she had gained weight; that little booty was now a big booty. My mind began to run wild, but I didn't trip— I was focused on this conversation we needed to have.

After two flights, we arrived at the island. I was already on edge about our conversation, but to add to that, we were there with her best friend, and my previous interactions with her hadn't gone well. I was concerned about how this would go; I didn't really know how she felt about me. But still, that would have to wait until after my wife and I talked.

We took a ferry to our side of the island, then took a cab to our rented condo. When we arrived, they told us our place wasn't ready and it would be an hour before we could check in. If we wanted, we could go sit in the villa clubhouse until our condo was ready. We agreed and proceeded toward the clubhouse.

Both of us were hungry from flying, so we decided to order food and drinks. As the cook prepared our food, we engaged in everyday conversation. Once the food was done, we ate and moved to the balcony. The view was beautiful; the sun was shining off the ocean, boats were floating, and people were riding jet skis. It created a very relaxing atmosphere. I asked her if she was ready to talk, and she replied yes.

She began to tell me about the hurt she had been holding inside. She told me how I had damaged her mentally and emotionally. As my wife gave her confession, tears began to roll down her face, and she began to sob, just thinking about everything I had done to her. She explained how her messaging another man began and what led her to that point. She expressed how she had felt like less of a human for years, how she had lost herself trying to please me. She had overworked herself to avoid being around me because I had shattered her heart as well.

For the first time in years, I was finally listening to my wife's cries. She had cried for so long right in front of me, and I had never heard her. She was finally able to tell me how she felt, with my ears open and my eyes paying attention. Watching her relieve herself reminded me of the hurt I had just experienced, and I thought to myself—she has forgiven me on so many occasions, so why can't I do the same?

The problem is that as men, we love to play games, but when the women grab the controller and score, we can't take it. But do we ever think, "Damn, I'm selfish?" or "I shouldn't be here?" Yeah, we do, but we figure, as long as she doesn't know and plays her part, we're good. But would we accept her cheating like us? Would we stand by her side after she's been caught? Would we accept, "I'm sorry, it won't happen again?" Most of us wouldn't; our pride would be too much. We'd be worried about what our friends would say and the image we have to maintain.

Life is a revolving door; it reflects what you throw at it, and karma loves to slap you in the face. Sometimes we have to feel pain in order to appreciate love, and sometimes we have to endure hurt to value the happiness we have with a person. Everyone has a heart; some of us just need that heart broken to remind us we're human too, and hurt has no specific victim—we can all be heartbroken.

So, I'm going to end this with this thought: If you love your woman, treat her like you do. Pay attention to her silent cries; listen when she's talking. She might need that ear or guidance, not only on how to live and handle situations in her life but also on how to be a better partner in your relationship. Always remember, hurt is a two-way street with no stop signs and no speed limits. We can all crash, but it's up to you to take another route. My wife and I are in a better place now because I finally understand her. Nothing's perfect, and everything takes work; it's a day-to-day learning experience. But we're holding on because deep inside we realized that we want this, and it's worth fighting for. No matter what, the past is the past, and we're not concentrating on what happened, but on what's happening now in our lives.

July 22, 2020

Today I'm feeling good. I woke up with a clear mind, no bad thoughts, and very peaceful. My wife and I are getting better, which gives me hope that we will succeed, and our past will be forgotten. Love is crazy—something I think no one will ever understand. It hurts; it makes you cry, but when you receive it, you feel as though nothing in this world could upset you. ☺

Push: ☹

No matter how hard I push, it's like she pulls away even harder. I tell myself that things will get better, but how long will that take? Sometimes it feels like we're moving forward, and sometimes we're not. I feel a distance, but I push it to the rear of my thoughts. Only God knows what our future looks like, and hopefully it's us together and happy. "Time will tell."

Hope:

Staying hopeful is what keeps me going. Life has thrown me a fair amount of curveballs, but I still manage to hit home runs. I've never given up on anything in life; I have always stood my ground with my head held high, fearing nothing—just having the willpower to win. However, love has instilled a fear in me. Everyone I've ever loved has always abandoned me and moved on as if I never mattered, and this feels the same. I might be overthinking, but my gut has never lied to me.

I've learned that you can change; you can correct your flaws for the sake of love. But none of that matters if the person you changed for doesn't know what they want or doesn't know how to accept the person they're asking you to become. So, at the end of the day, just make sure you like who you are becoming and that your changes are in your best interest, for your better future and success. If the person you changed for is truly ready and genuinely wants the perfect mate, they will start to sacrifice what they need to accommodate who you are becoming. They'll notice your growth and changes and begin their journey into becoming the mate you desire.

There is no "I" in team, nor in couple; it takes two to be successful in either. Just make sure you both have the same playbook or vision for how you want to make it together.

Things I Can Control
- My thoughts
- How I raise my boys
- My actions
- My future
- My anger

Things I Can't
- What people think
- How I'm treated
- What people say
- Love, tears, feelings, disappointment, fear, lies

The hardest part about forgiving is knowing the truth has been bent. A lot of things don't make sense to me; they just don't add up, making it hard to forget and forgive. I never thought I would find myself in this place of hurt. I never thought she would betray me and our marriage, and let's not forget our kids. September 14, 2019, was not only a day of marriage; it was the start of a promising future with the one person I knew would always have my back—the person for whom I sacrificed so much just to be the man she deserved. Now, it all feels like a waste. I love my wife, but I don't trust her.

It's funny how, as soon as we separated, this guy popped up. Either he has perfect timing, or this has been going on for a while. The way he stalks her and keeps trying to contact her makes me feel like there's more to the story. If he sent money, where's the proof? If it was only conversation, why is he so attached to her?

As I lay in bed at night, I look at the note I left for my wife and the picture I left on her dresser, and I ask myself: how could someone say they love you, lay in our bed in our home, and converse with another man? How could you look at our pictures and the note and still betray me?

I have built a wall around my heart, and it's going to take a construction team to break it down because every time I feel I've found the one, I always end up hurt and disappointed. I always lose and end up by myself. Being alone has always been my way of life by force; I fight, and my anger always gets the best of me. Why? Because all my life I've had to endure hurt, pain, betrayal, lies, deceit, and most of all, a broken heart. No one has ever truly loved me; I've never felt a part of any family. I've always been the outcast. I've always felt alone, and here I am again with the same feeling—just a different year and age.

When will I truly be loved? Will I ever be enough for people to accept? Will I ever have joy? Will I ever have a family that isn't tarnished?

The only way to forgive is through truth. The thing about truth is that it doesn't come in pieces; it doesn't have to be grilled out. The truth will flow like a river, while lies have potholes to dodge. So how do you forgive and move on when there are still secrets and lies? Your future will be built on lies and unforgiveness.

I have a lot of unanswered questions that will probably remain unanswered, but how can I forgive?

I love when my family sits together and watches movies. It reminds me of why I'm fighting and what I'm fighting for. It gives me peace and hope that everything will be okay. 😊

Why does she ask where I am before talking, and why does she have to wait until the headphones are on to converse? Something just doesn't add up. I've moved forward, letting go of the past so that my family can remain whole, but deep down, I know there's more to the story, and her friend is the answer. She knows everything she said at the time she felt she could do what she did. So, what else was done? What else did you feel you could do? I try hard not to think about it, but I'm only human, so my thoughts will always come. Those questions will always appear, no matter what.

Everybody is saying it's going to be alright, but when I'm so tired, my life has been a constant series of downfalls and letdowns. No one I trust can be trusted; no one I love deserves my love. I'm going back to who I am. Life was so much simpler. There's no one to love, which equals no one to hate.

WHAT IS LIFE WITHOUT PURPOSE, AND WHAT IS PURPOSE WITHOUT LIFE?

THE FINALE

THE FINALE

After all the changes and showing how much I love my wife, it doesn't matter. I've finally lost it all. I once told my wife that I had given her everything but my life. I see now that you have to die in order to live. This will be my last entry.

"To my boys, always remember how much fun we had; I really love you."

WHAT DO YOU DO WITH A DREAM AND NO LOVE?

WHO CAN I TRUST? NOBODY. 😣

… and I want you to know that Dad was just fighting a battle that I wasn't strong enough to beat. You probably won't understand, but one day you will understand.

"I love you, kids.

I love my family.

I love my wife.

But love couldn't save this.

Goodbye.

To Mom,

I know you're mad at me. How could I do this to you? I know. But, Ma, mentally, I've been damaged for years. I've never been able to love right, and not being able to love leaves me lonely and sad. That's been my life—

just sad and hiding it behind anger, trying not to show that I'm scared. I love you, but I had to find some peace. I had to; I was on the verge of a mental breakdown with a broken heart. Once again, hurt people hurt people, and I'm tired of doing that. I love you, "Fat Face."

"Tell my kids, 'Be strong. Don't cry. Be happy for me. I can finally rest, hurt-free, and that I love them and always will.'"

Back in here:

How did I get back here, hurt and feeling as if my world has ended? How did I get back here, confused, not knowing where I fit or if I fit in at all? How did I get back here, not sleeping, not really eating—just here? I went through this hurt before; I overcame it, so how did I end up back here?

I remember these sad days. No matter what goes on, I feel like I'm getting played with. I was finally accepting what she wanted, and I had found peace within. Now I'm back, and my love has grown, my feelings have attached, and once again, my heart hurts. My mind plays tricks on me; I can't sleep. I just feel she knew she didn't want me; she just likes to see me hurt because she's hurt. But if she's hurt and wasn't over it, why come back just to destroy me again?

She still plans as if I will be there to see them through, knowing she doesn't see me in her future. Deep down, she wants a fresh start—not with me, but fresh. I hurt, I cry, I plead, but nothing matters.

My brother said, "Bro, you ain't shit, and everything you touch, you destroy."

"Why plan with me when what you're planning isn't for me? Why allow me to get comfortable just to throw me away? -Hurt people hurt people."

My dreams have returned, and I've been sleeping well for a while, but I'm so tired of these dreams and the constant sadness. I feel like I'm losing it. I've never loved someone this way to the point where I have constant dreams of her leaving. Yesterday was her birthday; I didn't have much, but everything I had, I spent to make her smile.

As we were intimate, this was the second time she hasn't been fully present. She couldn't even stay engaged; you could tell her mind was somewhere else. I felt heartbroken to have my wife not into me. My heart has been in "hurt mode" ever since the day she said to me, "It's over." I experienced so much pain that day. Now my mind is tormenting me; my dreams are causing me pain, and I can't fight my thoughts.

I know I am going to hurt and that one day I may be hurt again. I trust her but fear her at the same time. She has my heart, and without a heart, how do you live? So, I'm scared.

"The hardest things to overcome are the easiest to grow from."

"I hate me
I Hatem
I hate life
I hate"

"I have to get myself together, but where do I start? I looked for a psychologist, and that door closed quickly. I have a little money coming in to help me get ahead, and trucking school will help, along with paying off my car. However, mentally, how do I release all the hurt and pain I've endured throughout my life? My trust is really messed up, which I know."

"If I die today who would care? NOBODY

Plans

1. Trucking school
2. Pay car off.
3. Find a hobby.
4. Take a trip.

PAIN

When pain comes, it hurts everything: the mind, the heart, the soul. It hurts so badly that it destroys your very being. Pain will play with your mind, leading you to sleepless nights. It will have you envisioning the questionable, overthinking the obvious, and feeling as if you're lost. Most people begin to be loners; we shy away to ourselves because it's easier to hide what we're going through. We become more and more disconnected from life and purpose. Pain can make you feel ready to take your life due to the fact that you're tired of feeling this way.

I know pain all too well, but I ask: why me? Why now? What is happiness? Does it exist? And why can't I have it? "So tired."

Love

Dear Love,

I don't understand you. How can you feel so amazing but hurt so badly? Remember when I told you I'd never trust you again? I meant that. Ever since I was younger, you've hurt me every time I trust you, and I'm in pain.

I always allow you to show me all my wants and needs. You trick me every time, and I fall for it. I fight hard, but the things you present feel so good that they blind me with love, making it hard to see the attack of lies, deceit, and disloyalty. I hate you so much because you hate me, but I want to be loved. How can I when love has hurt me the most? – Tears

"I can't leave my boys I made a promise."
"Sometimes life is just better off without you."

Dreams

For days, I haven't been sleeping well due to constant dreams of deception and disloyalty. She's lying because the only time I have dreams is when something isn't right. She said she dealt with the YouTube rapper to hurt me, so why wouldn't she sleep with the nigga I took her from? That would hurt the most. I'm trying to take it like a man, but the lies hurt more. My wife, my supposed best friend, doesn't even belong to me. I remember I caught them sending money to each other in 2019 but knowing that I was right about them makes me want blood.

She's not mine; she's her past: Love one woman.
She's a liar; her love is questionable.
She doesn't love me and never did.
She's sneaky.

Watch her; don't let your guard down to too many untold truths.

"Aint no future when past situations becoming present."

"Why can't I find the old me? Or am I not supposed to find him? I miss me—at least the parts where I didn't care about or love Shit."

It's been a week now, and the dreams won't stop. I haven't really gotten any sleep, but there's a reason they're coming like this. She's lying about something because the last time I had these dreams, I was right; my dreams never come unless something isn't right.

I don't know what's going on, but I do know it's going to hurt because the dreams hurt so badly. I just hope God protects me and gives me strength.

I'm losing this mental battle; it's making me want to leave this life. I watch her, and I don't see what I used to see.

I should have kept my guard up. I hate that I allowed myself to love. Now, this is one more wound I've added to the many I already had. "Fuck love."

I hope this money drops so I can make sure my son is okay because I can't keep fighting. I'm tired of crying, and I'm tired of hurting. Who wants to keep living a life full of disappointments? I'm going to get life insurance for them, so at least I leave them something other than a broken heart. I hope they will understand, but I've lost this fight—the battle I cannot win.

"Scared to get help Cuz I tried before and she was cheating while I was there."

"I should have killed that nigga and me too, and that way I wouldn't have to worry about her loving him or loving me."

"What if I inflicted the pain physically that I've received mentally? What if I just began to lash out and show my hurt through violence? Would I be wrong?"

Death, Hurt, Pain= Suicide
Suicide= Peace

Why didn't I just let go why did I fight to live?

Khi Khi & Lil Juan need mt but I hate me so do I live for them?

Promises

Next time I'm hurt, I'm going to make them and me famous. The world is gone to view my pain; the world is gone to feel my hurt—and those who have wronged me will feel my vengeance.

THE BREAKING POINT

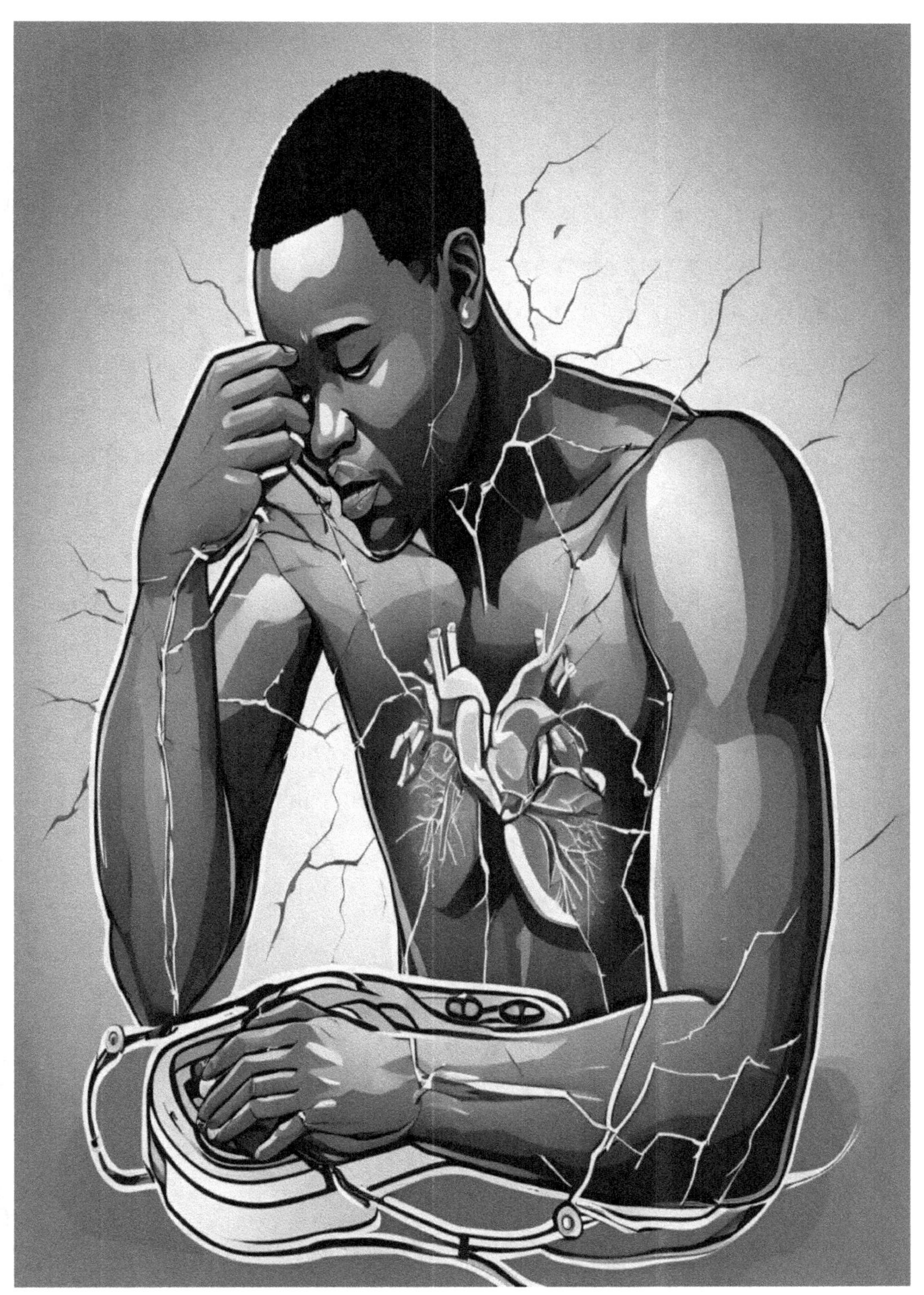

THE BREAKING POINT

One day I will lose this battle one day my thoughts will overcome me the sadness that I harbor will win and the ongoing thoughts of death will become my reality. I hide some much pain inside of me to where my body feels as if pain is normal my heart beats my lungs generate air but my soul is dead. I suppress my tears when they want to fall I laugh even when wanting to cry I say I'm ok knowing I'm far from it. Strong physical but mentally weak emotionally broken and internally damaged it's sad because no matter how hard I fight and how much love comes my way I still feel empty I still feel there's a void I'm missing I still feel as if I'm wrong for my actions if I'm truly stand firm on my oath before god how do you move forward when moving backwards is all you know how to do how do you plan when yours plan's consisted of people who you are no longer a value you too I'm scared naw I'm terrified of becoming close to anyone I know everyone ain't the same and everybody deserves a chance but dam I haven't even given me a chance I want death so bad but can't leave because I have promises I've made to my children my sons look up to me and would be lost without their father but how do I lead when I'm lost myself I awake every day and even tho the sun is out and it's a beautiful day all I see is darkness all I see is another day of suffering lord please guide me and help me make the decisions I cannot give me a gps to healing my mind and soul for I am lost and my only way I know Is to give up as a whole I honestly don't want to be here anymore but I'm trying I honestly don't want life anymore but I'm pushing my new friend is a help she has the faith that I need the guidance I look for and the strength tho help me build but I'm already too far gone 🖤💔

08/01/2024 will be my termination date.

May peace finally be mine and may my soul rest for the first time 

I have made my decision 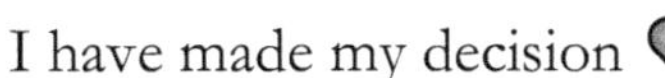

LETTING GO

LETTING GO

The hardest thing about walking away from someone you love is letting go. Although your actions may say you're done, your heart still holds love and honor for that person. When love is real and your heart was truly open, the thought of letting go stings with unbearable pain. Your mind races with thoughts of everything imaginable.

Learning to love someone is hard, and walking away is even harder—especially when you've devoted time and effort to that individual. When two people come together in an effort to build something, nobody plans for things to go sideways. Nobody prepares for the "what-ifs." We just focus on building and loving each other. Not once does it cross our minds, what if this doesn't work out? What if we're not meant to be?

To build with someone is a beautiful thing. Everyone wants that person who makes them feel complete. Everyone wants that forever love—the "make it last forever" kind. So, we search. We go through different relationships, different hurts, different pains, and most of all, different mental battles—searching and praying for that one somebody to love us for who we are, that one person to settle down with and enjoy life.

It's sad because, most of the time, by the time we meet someone even close to being that person, we're so broken that we can't even see the prize standing in front of us. We can't even fathom the thought of trusting someone new because we haven't let go of past disappointments. We haven't let go of the chance of reuniting with what once was, holding on to the "what-ifs" and possibilities. We haven't let go of the memories and plans we once made in our past relationship.

So how do you let go of someone you never intended to release? How do you let go of someone you still wish to hold? How do you erase years of invested time? How do you keep trying to love someone who has no plans of accepting your love, who chooses to ignore your love languages, and who isn't willing to sacrifice any of their ways to accommodate yours?

They say anything worth having is worth fighting for, but what we fail to realize is that it's only a fight when both parties are in the ring. Yes, the man may be the leader of the household, and he may be the head, but I've never seen a head work properly without a strong neck. The woman is the neck. Even though a man may run the house, the woman sets the tone— she shapes the outcome of all situations. A man can provide and protect, but he can't nurture the home as a woman would, just as a woman couldn't protect the home as her man could.

Relationships are built between two imperfect people striving to grow— not just for the longevity of the relationship, but for each other. It's two people coming together in harmony, open to learning and understanding one another. With that comes miscommunication and testing times that only love can keep together.

So, what is letting go? In all honesty, you never truly do. You just learn to accept what cannot be. You learn to endure the hurt and pain of a failed attempt and live with the experience of knowing what love is and how it felt.

Just because you plant a seed in the soil doesn't mean the soil will produce the flowers you anticipated. It doesn't mean you will have a beautiful garden. You may water the seed, feed it all its nutrients, and nurture it to the best of your ability, but if the soil is no longer willing to produce, no matter what you do, that seed will never grow.

So never say you're letting go, because in truth, you're holding on. Everything you went through has shown you what you will not tolerate or accept in your future. It has shown you strength where you thought you were weak. It has shown you that you can still love in the midst of hate. It has shown you loyalty as well as disloyalty. And most of all, it has shown you how to rebuild your heart after it's been shattered.

Never let go—just rebuild. And this time, take your time. Pay attention to the small things. Pay attention to the unseen or unspoken emotions of your partner. Let the act of not letting go build you.

Hurt builds character, pain builds strength, miscommunication builds communication, and losses build wins. 💯

MISGUIDED INTENTIONS

MISGUIDED INTENTIONS

The word love is used every day, often with no true feelings behind it. Hearts are misguided simply by hearing that one word—love. Minds and thoughts become distorted due to wrongful accusations disguised by the phrase, I love you.

Love is a word that has destroyed so many hearts and lives—a word with such a strong meaning but used as if it had none. Lyfe Jennings said in a song that he was taught love was supposed to feel like hate. But why is this?

Is it because everyone wants to be loved wholeheartedly, and in their yearning, they show the love they wish to receive? Is it because they give this love to people who don't even recognize it? Perhaps the love they are showing isn't love at all—maybe the love they are giving is, in truth, a form of hate.

STICKING TO MYSELF

STICKING TO MYSELF

I've got to let my broken heart heal. Tired of the lies and fake love—they say it's real, but their love is based on what you give. Misguided love wasn't part of the deal.

Low on trust, love, and belief—can I get a refill? Shamed and character assassinated by those closest to me. Outcast and abandoned by those who were supposed to support me.

Lost in thought daily because I don't even know myself anymore. I lost who I was trying to get people to understand me. Now I sit here, just a vessel with no plan B. Every thought and passion I had was planned around my family.

Damn, what a reality. The same people I let on my boat were trying to sink me, sabotaging every move I made just to hurt me. Revengeful hearts and secret conversations I couldn't hear or see.

It's okay, because God's got me.

Damn, what a reality.

MY TRUTH

MY TRUTH

After months of trying to rekindle my relationship with my wife—months of begging, pleading, and constant rejection of my advances—I had tried everything. I bought her gifts, planned dates, and tried to have heartfelt conversations. I even told her that if she had been with someone else, it didn't matter as long as she came back home. Nothing worked. She continued with her antics, ignoring me and living her life as if nothing I said or did meant anything.

Each day, I was tormented. I was so close to the one woman I had ever loved this deeply, yet she wouldn't give me the time of day. She wouldn't acknowledge my feelings or care about the mental battle that was defeating me in the worst way. She'd call me after going to clubs, telling me how men were all over her, trying to get her number. She'd send pictures of how she was dressed, leaving my mind racing and my heart pounding. She often posted pictures on social media of herself at clubs with new friends, captioning them with statuses like, "When you tell a man you're done, now they're hurting."

She was showing me all the signs of a woman who no longer wanted her man. She was living a single life, while I was trapped fighting a legal battle that could cost me 22 years in prison—a case she had given me up on. My life was unraveling. I'd lost my job, my freedom (on electronic monitoring), and almost everything I owned. My rent was barely getting paid, and food was scarce.

Despite everything, I never resorted to taking from anyone. There were days she brought me food from her home or went grocery shopping for me—I give her credit for that. But I sat in my house for months, drinking heavily, and eventually turned to drugs—cocaine and ecstasy pills—just to numb the pain. The spiral was unstoppable.

A few weeks into house arrest, the judge lifted the restriction. I found a new job and started counseling, trying to claw my way back. But the devil never stops. One day, on the way to work, I received discovery documents from my attorney. As I read them, my world shattered. In black and white, I saw everything she had told authorities—claims of stalking, accusations of weapons, and lies about how she made me leave our home a year earlier. She painted me as a monster, and even my children had corroborated these falsehoods.

The betrayal crushed me. Driving to work, my heart raced, my mind spun, and tears flowed uncontrollably. The pain became unbearable, and before I knew it, I blacked out. When I regained consciousness, I had crashed into the trailer of a truck. Stumbling out of the car, I was disoriented but physically unharmed. The driver of the other vehicle checked on me and moved his truck, leaving me to assess the damage. My car was totaled—the last thing I had of value.

I called my mom, who went into a panic but managed to calm me. She warned me that this situation was destroying me and told me to get it together. I called my wife for help, and she came to the scene. She asked if I needed a doctor, but I refused—I couldn't afford it. After finding a tow truck with help from my mom, my wife left. As she walked away, I sat there, still reeling from what I had read in the discovery.

The tow truck driver dropped me at home, and I called my job to explain the situation. Since I had just started the job through a temp agency, they let me go immediately. Defeated didn't even begin to describe how I felt. My life was spiraling out of control, and I couldn't see a way out.

I cried for hours, asking God why He was punishing me. I felt broken and contemplated suicide. Everything I had built was gone, and I couldn't understand why. My mom tried to console me with a story from the Bible about a man who lost it all but was redeemed by God. Her words helped momentarily, but the pain remained.

I called my wife and tried to explain how I felt about our situation and my struggles. I told her I wanted my family back, that nothing else mattered—not the lies or infidelities. Her response broke me further. She said, "Jajuan, I have nothing else for you. The person I was for you, I can no longer be. You want me to comfort you, but I can't. You want this family back? Show us. But I can't help you with anything beyond mental support."

Her words, "Show us," echoed in my mind. What more could I show? I had left Chicago, sacrificed everything, sold my possessions, and even donated plasma to keep us afloat. I had done everything to prove my love and commitment, yet it was never enough.

From that moment, I knew I had to focus on myself. It's heartbreaking how many men dedicate their lives to their families, only to realize they were an option, not a priority. For weeks, I stayed to myself, trying to heal and rebuild my confidence.

During this time, an old friend reached out after hearing about my struggles. She spoke life into me, reminding me of my worth. She supported me in every way—sending self-help books, helping with my bills, and encouraging me daily. She poured love and positivity into me without expecting anything in return.

Slowly, I began to heal. I found a new job, started working out, and spent time with my sons. Life started to turn around, and I began feeling like myself again. That's when my wife noticed the change—how I kept money in my pocket, how my sons had new shoes, and how I was no longer affected by her actions.

She started to reach out, asking for help and favors. Despite everything she had done, I gave when she asked and showed up when she needed. For her birthday, I even treated her to a nice dinner and bought her a gift. People might call me crazy or tenderhearted, but I loved this woman deeply, and no matter how much she hurt me, I continued to show her love.

God doesn't judge us by how others treat us but by how we treat others. I've always believed in giving, especially to those I love. Yet, no matter how much I gave, it was never enough. Every gesture of kindness was met with arguments and chaos.

In the end, I had to fall back and focus on myself and my kids. It was time to let go of what wasn't meant for me and rebuild the life I deserved.

UNANSWERED QUESTIONS

UNANSWERED QUESTIONS

How many days do I have to wait for you?

How many days do I have to be lonely, longing for your presence?

How many ways am I supposed to show you I love you?

How many times must I sit and wait for you to realize that I'm here?

How long am I supposed to wait for you to want me—for you to want us?

Why do I have to wait if love is truly in your heart?

Why are we enemies?

Why do you hate me when you're the one who has mishandled me?

Why did it take me becoming friends with another woman for you to notice me?

How long was I supposed to hurt for you, while you didn't care?

Why don't my feelings count, yet yours are always a priority in my day-to-day life?

Why couldn't you just love me the way I loved you?

Why, if our family was so important, did you push me out?

This is the second time you've committed these acts—how many more times am I supposed to allow you to do as you please and return when you're done?

Why marry me if you still had open wounds from past experiences?

IS IT MY FAULT?

IS IT MY FAULT?

I'm sitting here deep in thought. My son hasn't been himself since his mom and I went our separate ways. I noticed the change months ago. I saw how he started acting out and even paid attention to how he carried himself around me.

My son has witnessed so much in his life—me and his mom fighting, me being put in cuffs. He's stood and watched as I fought my depression. He's seen me cry, seen me smile, and even witnessed me give up.

My little best friend. I remember the day he was born. I walked into the baby room and asked if I could hold him. He was so small, and I was so scared because he was my first child. I had never been a father before. As I held him, tears came to my eyes. I lifted him up so that his ear was by my mouth, and I said to him, "No matter what comes my way, I will never leave your side. I promise."

While raising him, I always reminded him of that day, reassuring him that I would always stand by those words. I remember one evening when I was having a breakdown. My son walked up to me and hugged me. He looked into my eyes and said, "Dad, remember your promise. Remember you'll never leave me." Then he added, "And Dad, I'll never leave you." My little rider.

Me and my son have always been best friends. We talk about everything. He gives me light when all I see is darkness. My junior. But now, he's having the hardest time trying to adjust to this new life where I'm not there with him.

Damn.

DO WE?

DO WE?

It's been a long journey—a lot of ups and downs, a lot of betrayal, disappointments, and disagreements. It's been filled with lies, misguided love, and pain.

Here we are now, facing our second separation in four years of marriage. The second time breaking up our home. The second time putting our kids through a battle. Their unspoken pain shows.

The second time saying we need space, acknowledging that both our minds are traumatized from past experiences and the damage we've inflicted on each other feels like too much to handle.

You say I love too hard.
I say you don't love enough.
You say I'm too overprotective.
I say I'm just trying to keep you safe.
You say I don't listen to you.
I say you don't see me.
You say I'm the same man you met years ago.
I say I'm not, and my actions prove it.
You say I have anger issues.
I say I don't—I just have a low tolerance for B.S.
You say you love me with all your heart.
I say I don't feel like your heart beats for me anymore.

We both have our own opinions about our love, our pain, and our hurt. But if you really pay attention, you'll notice something missing: we never say what we love about each other.

We never acknowledge the good in us or in our relationship. Instead, we continue to bring up past dramas, past actions, and old feelings. We separate time and time again because we both carry insecurities, trust issues, and unspoken truths.

Uncomfortable conversations—that's what we lack. Our inability to accept and move on is what hinders our growth. We point fingers, playing the victim, when in reality, we're both doing the same things.

Neither of us is building—we're both tearing down. We build, then destroy. We build, then tear down again. We build, only to decide we don't like what we've created.

We are our own worst enemies.

Instead of being a team, we've become opponents. Instead of lifting each other up, we tear each other down—mentally and emotionally. And then we wonder why we keep ending up apart.

In reality, we're both lost—trapped in a place where we don't want to say goodbye because we know each other's value, but we can't move forward because we can't see past what has been done or said.

I say all this to ask: do we really know each other?

I REMEMBER

I REMEMBER

It's crazy how people can sit and bash you, call you the devil, say you're a bag of trash and a downfall. But I remember.

I remember when I first met you. We were two broken young adults who had faced some of the harshest realities life could throw at us. I remember sitting on the porch all night, listening to you tell me your dreams and nightmares—all in the same breath.

I remember arguing with your family about whether my child was mine or not because, in their eyes, you were a whore who couldn't be trusted. I remember when the same woman who now bashes me and says I wasn't shit put you and your two daughters out in the cold. I begged my mom to let you stay with us.

I remember us lying on that hardwood floor with one blanket, a sheet, and two pillows to share among the four of us. I also remember the fights and arguments. I remember the choking, the slaps—and yes, I remember the days I cheated, the nights I stayed out and came home late. Things weren't always pretty or calm. But I also remember when you fought for me.

I remember when we moved up north with nothing. Your mom gave us her old furniture. I remember going out on the block trying to sell dope so my son could have his first birthday party. I remember how cold those cuffs were when I got caught trying to provide for y'all. I remember you sitting in the car with an unknown amount of heroin, not knowing what to do because the police had taken me.

I remember sitting in that cell, receiving letters and pictures from you. On visiting days, I could count on you to be there. I remember calling you and hearing that our place had been broken into and the car had been wrecked. I remember coming home, and once again, it was us and now our three children back on the floor.

I remember our struggle—how hard it was for us. I remember the same people who talk about us now never reaching out to help, yet secretly disclosing everything we were going through and laughing at our downfall.

I remember that Thanksgiving when I wore sandals in the snow just to make sure our kids looked good. I remember lying on that bed, watching as plasma was drawn from my body, just so I could feed our kids—and you—for the night, even if it meant I didn't eat.

I remember the plans we made while we were broke. How we dreamed of owning a house, cars, and sending our kids to good schools where they'd play sports. I remember the day I asked for your hand in marriage. We were so broke that I made an engagement ring out of aluminum foil and placed a diamond earring in the middle.

I remember singing Joe's "Priceless" to you in front of my family on Christmas morning. I remember telling you, "I might not have the money right now to give you the ring you deserve, but if you say yes, I promise

I'll get it for you." I remember how you smiled and cried at the same time while saying yes—you would be my wife, my forever girl.

I remember. Not just the good, but the bad.

Dammit, I remember!

WHAT I WANT, IS WHAT I ALWAYS WANTED "YOU"

WHAT I WANT, IS WHAT I ALWAYS WANTED "YOU"

You asked me what I wanted from you. I've been stuck on that question for a while, but now I have the answers.

I want to feel secure again. I remember when I had nothing—fresh out of jail, no clothes, no fancy shoes, just me. No money, no car—just me. And you made me feel unstoppable.

I want to feel that love again. I remember watching you walk toward me down that walkway. The way my heartbeat—that was the first time I truly felt it. I remember the emotions that ran through my body—both happy and nervous. But I knew I had made the right choice.

I want to feel wanted again. I remember how you used to look at me with fire in your eyes, how you always wanted me around, how you would catch the bus to my house just to be in my presence.

I want to trust your love without worrying that, if things aren't perfect, your love will change again. Will you run away, or will you stay and fight it out?

I want to feel whole. Right now, I feel like half a man. Why? Because of my situation and the fact that I'm not with my family. There are too many memories, too many years, to give up. But sometimes, I feel like you don't understand me, like my feelings don't count.

I feel like you care, but you don't care. You love me, but your love feels watered down. Yes, I know my current situation is hard to deal with, and yes, I know it may hurt you. But how do you think I felt losing everything I worked for? How do you think I feel sleeping somewhere other than my own home or by your side?

No one can replace you. Yes, I wish I had done things differently. Yes, I wish I'd had the revenue to handle things better. Keisha, I've been broke for a while. My pride wouldn't let me tell you, and I was ashamed because of how I treated you while I was grinding.

Sure, I might have been there for you when you asked, but emotionally, I dropped the ball. Ask my son—I cried daily longing for you. I sat by myself most of the time, thinking about you. I just wish I could have come home to you. I wish we could have let go of our hurts and focused more on rebuilding our relationship.

Yes, marriages go through ups and downs, and yes, only the strong survive. But I feel like we forgot about each other and what made us say "I do."

I apologize for my actions toward you and for the situation I'm in. Just know that I still love the ground you walk on, and nothing or nobody can change that.

You're the first woman I ever loved, the first woman to give me children, the first woman to make me want to change. I know it might be hard to believe, but it's the truth.

You think I'm out here living my best life, but the whole time, I'm wanting you—wishing you would just say, "Jajuan, enough is enough. Come home." But I never get that call.

I might get bashed for trying to stay near you, for trying to keep a roof over my head. Keisha, I could have left a month ago—my probation was willing to approve it. But I can't leave y'all here. I'd rather struggle to make it than give up.

Hopefully, you understand what I'm saying and stop being so hard on me. I'm trying. This wasn't meant to hurt you or push you away. I love you with all of me, and I hope one day you'll see that no matter the sacrifice, no matter the pain or hurt, I will always choose to fight for you.

LOST AFTER LOST

LOST AFTER LOST

Hearing that my twins might not make it did something to me. I became angry and sad at the same time. I looked at the mother—the same mother I had been urging for months to go to the hospital, to get her medical card. I even fell out with her over it. And now, here she was, telling me something was going wrong with her pregnancy.

I don't feel any remorse for my anger because I knew something wasn't right. I saw how she wasn't growing. Her stomach never developed the way it should, and I asked countless times for her to get checked. I know there are strong women out here who don't like listening to a man, but when his concerns are about your well-being and that of your children, wouldn't it be worth considering? She could have been more accepting.

Now I sit here, not knowing the outcome. After burying a son and losing two people close to me, my twins were my light. I would sit for hours picturing how I'd treat my first little girl or how I'd have them dressed. I found joy in those thoughts.

I left the house because my anger toward her was starting to show. I felt like she was doing everything for everyone else except the ones who needed her most. It felt intentional. My feelings for her and my view of her started to change. She'll never understand why I left. She might even refrain from contacting me.

But I'm a real father. I take my kids seriously. I'm tired of not being listened to. I'm tired of the "nobody can tell me anything" attitude. I'm tired of the threats of losing her. I'm tired of people in general acting like I depend on them, as if their mere presence defines my worth. For years, I held my tongue out of fear of being alone. For years, I didn't speak up about the things that bothered me. For years, I walked around in pain, silenced by those who claimed to love and understand me.

Now, I sit here in this hotel room, trying to figure out my next move. I can't go home because of probation. Me and my ex-wife aren't on the best of terms. I dropped all my female friends when I started talking to her. Yeah, it's lonely, but I'd rather be lonely than unheard.

I just hope God protects my twins because they don't deserve to suffer or not live because of misunderstanding and a lack of listening. I hope God protects her. I hope God protects me. I don't know where this road is leading, but I'll travel it—with my head high, chest out, and praying.

A man can only be a man to a woman who accepts his thoughts, just as a father can only protect his children if their mother is willing to hear his opinions on their well-being and safety. 🙏

Conclusion

They say a man ant supposed to cry, but that couldn't be further from the truth. As you've read, I'm a man, and I've cried. I've been broken, I've loved, I've healed, and I've learned to say sorry. Let me tell you this from one man to another: it's okay. It's okay to cry. It's okay to feel broken. It's okay to love, to heal, and to make amends. Trust me—it's okay.

What's life if you walk around carrying built-up hurt and pain with no outlet? Now that I've let you into parts of my life, my hope is that my truth inspires you to walk into your own truth. I hope it helps you release the pain that's been holding you hostage.

I've never written a book before. Shit, I never thought I had it in me. But look at how life works out when you take a chance and step into the ring. The hardest part is showing up. The hardest part of any fight is just showing up. But if you show up and put your hands up, you've already won.

If you're reading these words today, it proves one thing: you didn't give up. And for that, I'm proud of you. Keep showing up. Keep fighting. Keep believing. In my book, you've already won.